Tarpeia

Salomon Reinach

Kessinger Publishing's Rare Reprints

Thousands of Scarce and Hard-to-Find Books on These and other Subjects!

- Americana
- Ancient Mysteries
- Animals
- Anthropology
- Architecture
- Arts
- Astrology
- Bibliographies
- Biographies & Memoirs
- Body, Mind & Spirit
- Business & Investing
- Children & Young Adult
- Collectibles
- Comparative Religions
- Crafts & Hobbies
- Earth Sciences
- Education
- Ephemera
- Fiction
- Folklore
- Geography
- Health & Diet
- History
- Hobbies & Leisure
- Humor
- Illustrated Books
- Language & Culture
- Law
- Life Sciences
- Literature
- Medicine & Pharmacy
- Metaphysical
- Music
- Mystery & Crime
- Mythology
- Natural History
- Outdoor & Nature
- Philosophy
- Poetry
- Political Science
- Science
- Psychiatry & Psychology
- Reference
- Religion & Spiritualism
- Rhetoric
- Sacred Books
- Science Fiction
- Science & Technology
- Self-Help
- Social Sciences
- Symbolism
- Theatre & Drama
- Theology
- Travel & Explorations
- War & Military
- Women
- Yoga
- *Plus Much More!*

We kindly invite you to view our catalog list at:
http://www.kessinger.net

CHAPTER IV

TARPEIA [1]

I

' WHY,' asks Plutarch in the thirty-seventh chapter of his
' Roman Questions,' 'should custom have ordained that,
out of all the offerings we make to heaven, only the spoils
of war should be left to the mercies of moth and rust,
untended and unrepaired ?'[2]   Plutarch's questions are
invariably of great interest, for the simple reason that
they hinge upon customs to which his age had lost the
clue. Plutarch's answers, however, are usually absurd,
for the equally simple reason that he brings to the inter-
pretation of prehistoric religious usage the intellectual
stock-in-trade of a philosophic amateur in the first century
after Christ. In the present instance, he hazards two
solutions of the problem. Either the disappearance of
the spoils would dim the splendour of the exploits com-
memorated, and spur another generation to fresh feats
of arms ; or, on the other hand, there might be something odious in the notion of perpetuating the memory

---

[1] *Revue archéologique*, 1908, i. pp. 42–74.
[2] Plut. *Quaest. Rom.* c. 37, p. 237e.   The text is uncertain on one
point (προσκυνεῖν in the sense of ' taking care ') ; but the general sense
is not in doubt.

of spilt blood and stricken fields—precisely as Greek opinion deplored the audacity which first reared trophies in stone or bronze.[1] . . . These specimens of exegesis speak for themselves : comment would be out of place.

To-day the question raised by Plutarch is one of a class which the science of comparative religion and custom is able to answer off-hand : if the Romans did not repair their trophies, it was because those trophies were invested with a sanctity of their own which rendered all contact perilous. The Hebrew Ark of the Covenant, to go no further, is a case in point, though with this difference : the sanctity of the Ark was inherent in its origin, while the sanctity of spoils wrested from the enemy was an adventitious result of the circumstances which caused them to change hands after the combat.

II

Among the early Romans, who erected no trophies on the field of battle,[2] we find the spoils hung in temples and public buildings, in private houses and on trees—particularly oaks. This last mode of exposure, to which both Virgil and Statius allude,[3] is obviously the first in point of time. Nor had its memory passed away in the first century of the Empire ; witness the famous passage [4] where Lucan compares Pompey to an old and leafless oak, long dead, which, standing in the midst of a fruitful field and charged with ancient spoils, still remains an

---

[1] *Cf.* Cic. *De Invent.* ii. 23, 69 ; Diod. Sic. xiii. 24 ; Plut. *Alcib.* 29. The use of metal trophies was general later on in Greece ; but the Macedonians never raised trophies of any sort (Paus. ix. 40, 9).

[2] Florus, iii. 2.

[3] Virg. *Aen.* xi. 5 *sqq.* ; Stat. *Theb.* ii. 707 *sqq.*

[4] Lucan, *Phars.* i. 136 *sqq.*

object of adoration. Now, if a tree like this—whose age was to be counted by centuries—could stand in the very heart of the countryside, braving the casual cupidity of every passer-by, and yet retain its burden inviolate, there is only one conclusion to be drawn : the spoils were protected from all contact by the sanctity attached to them. Conversely, if these were left to hang on the withered boughs of a tottering oak, and not a man dreamt of transferring them to a sounder stem, it can only have been because the support of the spoils was as sacred as the spoils themselves. Only the natural chances of time and tide could reduce them to dust : the hand of man must on no account interfere in the process.

Equally intangible, in the strict sense of the word, were the private trophies in the home of a successful commander. Generation after generation they hung secure from injury—patents of nobility to the house, and sources of prestige to its owner.[1] So, after the disaster at Cannae, when Fabius wished to fill up the gaps hewn in the senatorial ranks, he chose a certain number of burgesses whose family residences were ornamented with spoil stripped from the enemy.[2] Pompey's house— *rostrata domus*—was still gay with the prows of Cilician ships when it passed to Mark Antony, and later, by inheritance, to a forbear of the emperor Gordian.[3] In the great fire under Nero, Suetonius tells us, the mansions of old-world generals perished ' still ornamented with

---

[1] ' They arrange their trophies,' says Polybius (vi. 39), ' in the most conspicuous positions available, as they consider them palpable evidence of their own prowess.' Similarly, Tibullus (i. 1, 54) admits it may well become Messala to war by sea and land, ' that his house may flaunt it in hostile spoils.' Compare also Liv. x. 7 ; Cic. *Phil.* ii. 28 ; Sil. It. *Pun.* vi. 436, &c.

[2] Liv. xxiii. 23 : ' qui spolia ex hoste fixa domi haberent.'

[3] Capitolinus, *Gordian*, 3 ; *cf.* Cic. *Phil.* ii. 28, 68.

the enemies' spoils.'[1] Even when a house passed by sale to another family, the new owner might not touch the *spolia*, still less remove them.[2] There is a shade of guilelessness in the notion that this prohibition of touching, tending or repairing the *spolia* was dictated by fear lest the unscrupulous should display apocryphal spoil in their houses—much as old armour or family portraits are bought at a price to-day.[3] The scruple, proof of which we have already adduced, was purely religious, and the Romans continued to act in conformity with it long after they had lost all real comprehension of its character.

In the temples—the habitation of the gods—the trophies were nailed on the walls and could never be removed. Only in circumstances of the utmost gravity, when the salvation of the state hung by a thread, was it permissible to equip recruits with the arms of a vanquished enemy. After Cannae, at a moment when Rome appeared defenceless, the consuls, according to Livy, had weapons made in hot haste, and ' the spoils of ancient foemen were torn down from temple and portico.'[4] A little later the dictator M. Junius Pera was authorised by special edict to mount on horseback,—this was contrary to religious law,—and proceeded to accoutre six thousand men in the Gaulish arms which had decked the triumph of Flaminius.[5] Livy well knew that such a measure was every whit as exceptional as the other which was passed at the same time and opened the ranks of the Roman army to slaves. They were, he says, ' the last resources

---

[1] Suet. *Nero*, 38 : ' hostilibus adhuc spoliis ornatae.'

[2] Pliny, xxxv. 7.

[3] 'The object being doubtless to guard against the frauds of false pretenders.' Smith, *Dict. of Ant.*, s.v. ' Spolia,' p. 691.

[4] Liv. xxii. 57.   [5] *Ibid.* xxiii. 14.

of an almost desperate state, driven to make convention give way to necessity.'[1]   The use of arms taken in war was so abnormal a course that it was only adopted with hesitancy, even if the spoils were not the fruits of victory, but a gift.   During the revolt of Syracuse, Livy relates, 'the armed citizens mustered in the public squares, while the unarmed flocked to the shrine of Olympian Jove in search of the Gallic and Illyrian spoils which Rome had bequeathed to Hiero.   Let Heaven be gracious, they prayed, and lend them these sacred arms ; every blow they struck should be for fatherland, for freedom, and for the temples of their gods.'[2]   The arms were indeed sacred, but not more so than those in the porticoes and private houses of Rome.   The point was, not that they belonged to a temple, but that they were arms taken in war—*exuviae*.   By the very fact of their capture they were withdrawn from use, and became—theoretically, at least—untouchable ; just as we have seen to be the case when they simply hung on tree-branches or house-walls. The religious character of the temples where they were lodged added nothing to the sanctity inherent in them ; the most it could do was to guarantee that sanctity by rendering it apparent to all eyes.

III

This example, after so many others, shows the perversity of certain historians, still inspired by the prejudices of the eighteenth century, who seek in public utility—or what we are now pleased to consider such—

---

[1] 'Honesta utilibus cedunt' (Liv. xxiii. 14, 3).   *Cf.* the speech of Fabius in the *Punica* of Silius, x. 598 *sqq.*

[2] Livy, xxxiv. 21.

the origin of primeval law and custom. Two poverty-
stricken tribes go to war ; an engagement is fought, and
the victors collect the arms and clothing of the vanquished.
Common sense, a bad guide for once, would say they were
making hay while the sun shone, in order to follow up an
initial success with fresh resources. Unfortunately, the
winning tribe does nothing of the sort, unless driven
by an absolute necessity which silences the scruples of
religion. The spoils are sacred, and must be called in
from circulation because they have become dangerous to
touch. Sometimes, as we have seen, they may be hung
out of reach in a building : sometimes, and this earlier—
for man makes war long before temples, porticoes, and
houses—they may be thrown into water, or destroyed by
fire. Finally, if the tribe is sedentary, they may be
piled upon a consecrated part of its territory, with the
prohibition attached that none shall lay a hand on them.
In short, the rites prescribed for the treatment of spoils
correspond to the various funerary rites—suspension in
mid-air until the slow process of natural decay is com-
plete, immersion, cremation, burial. The four elements,
air, water, fire, and earth, combine to rescue man from
the dangers—not of this world—with which he is
threatened by the sacred objects. In the course of time,
thanks to the priesthood whose business it is to conciliate
or neutralise the powers of magic, we find the work of
destruction arrested. Man no longer sequestrates the
whole of his capture from the usages of life, he surrenders
a fraction to the gods—in other words, to the priests who
allow him to dispose of the remainder at will. The bulk
of what were *spoils* has become *booty*. And yet on the
ever valid principle of the survival of religious scruples,
the spoils taken from an enemy have never entirely lost

the sacred character with which they were originally invested ; there has always been a shade of reluctance to treat them as everyday objects available for any purpose. At a period when first-fruits and tithes of the booty were no longer offered to heaven, Napoleon had the cannon captured by the Grande Armée cast into a triumphal column, instead of adding them to his batteries or keeping them in his arsenals to fight another day.

IV

We have spoken of the destruction of spoils by fire, of their immersion in water, of their exposure on land ; we have now to collect a few examples of these primitive rites.

Orosius, probably on the authority of Livy,[1] states that the Cimbrians and Teutons, after routing the consul Manilius and the proconsul Caepio, destroyed the whole of the immense booty which they seized in the two Roman camps. Articles of clothing were torn to shreds and scattered to the winds ; gold and silver were flung into the river, horses into an abyss ; the equipment of men and chargers was broken up piecemeal. In the conduct of these barbarians—' extravagant ' he naturally considers it—Orosius sees ' a new and unusual mode of execration.' [2] To the Danish scholars of the nineteenth century, Worsaae in particular, belongs the credit of proving that here we have nothing either ' new ' or ' unusual ' ; only the simple performance of a rite familiar to the barbarian peoples of the North. In 1866 Worsaae thus explained the numerous finds of bronze weapons and ornaments

[1] Orosius, v. 16.
[2] '. . . nova quadam atque insolita execratione.'

E

in the turf-pits of Denmark, which actually are old lakes ; a year later he extended his theory to the Bronze Age.[1] 'In all the deposits from our turf-pits,' said Engelhardt at the Congress of Copenhagen (1869),[2] ' there is hardly a single object but is imperfect, and unfitted for subsequent use. . . . The fact is, all these deposits come from booty collected on the field of battle and the articles have been deliberately incapacitated during the process of offering them to the gods, to whom a sacrifice of this nature had been promised beforehand : the warriors kept nothing but the glory. The passages cited by Worsaae and Beauvois from a number of classical authors, together with Steenstrup's profound study of the animal bones found in the same strata as the antiquities, and mixed with them, have thoroughly cleared up this point, which but lately seemed inexplicable.'

Worsaae's theory was popularised in France by Alexandre Bertrand, who wrote an article on the subject, under the title ' La Part des dieux.' [3]   His monograph, like those of Worsaae which it recapitulates, is marred by several anachronisms ;   indeed, the title—felicitous though it may seem—is itself one. In the days when Rome had evolved her polytheistic system, and religious customs of the kind we are dealing with had already a grey antiquity behind them, the classical writers believed that the spoils destroyed or abandoned were vowed to certain divinities or reduced to nothingness in their honour.   Livy has several references to spoils burnt ' to

[1] Worsaae, *Mém. de la Soc. des antiquaires du Nord*, 1866, p. 61 ; cf. O. Tischler, *Gedächtnissrede an Worsaae*, 1886, p. 8.

[2] *Congrès d'archéol. préhistorique* (Copenhagen), 1869, p. 200.

[3] August 5, 1872.   See Bertrand, *Archéol. celtique et gauloise*, ed. 2, p. 221.   Cf. S. Müller, *Mém. de la Soc. des antiquaires du Nord*, 1884–1889, p. 225.

Vulcan '—*spolia Vulcano cremantur*.[1] Elsewhere we find spoils vowed to Jupiter, Mars, Lua Mater, ' and the other gods to whom religion permits the consecration by fire of hostile spoils.' [2] It was to Mars, Minerva, Lua, and the rest of the gods that Aemilius Paulus solemnly addressed himself, when, after having the shields of brass transported on his galleys, he heaped together the other arms of every description, fired the pile with his own hands, and invited the military tribunes to throw lighted torches upon it. In conforming to this archaic ritual, Paulus believed—or feigned to believe—that he was burning the Macedonian arms *in honour of the gods*; in reality, he was following a venerable custom of earlier date than the constitution of the Roman Pantheon. Of all the divinities whom Livy names in similar circumstances, one only had not been hellenised in the time of Aemilius Paulus : this was *Lua*, whose name is related to *lues*, and means purely and simply *destruction*. To vow to Lua is to destroy, and nothing else. To recognise the ' portion of the gods ' in sacrifices of this type is all the less legitimate because the accredited representatives of the gods, the priests, received nothing. If every offering to Vulcan had been necessarily burnt, his temple would never have contained anything but ashes. The portion of the gods was not the part destroyed, but, on the contrary, the part preserved ; and the victor could only have made his offering in the relatively late era when there were temples to hold it and priests to receive it. True, Livy relates that Romulus, after the defeat of Acron, whom he killed and stripped of

---

[1] Liv. i. 37 ; viii. 10 ; xxiii. 46 ; xxx. 6 ; xli. 2 ; *cf.* Preller-Jordan, *Röm. Mythologie*, ii. p. 162.

[2] Liv. x. 29, ' Iovi victori spolia cum vovisset . . . cremavit ': *ibid.* xlv. 33, ' Marti, Minervae, Luaeque Matri et ceteris deis quibus spolia hostium dicare fas est succensi.'

E 2

his arms, consecrated the spoil of that chief in the temple
of Jupiter Feretrius, so called from the litter or *feretrum*
used for the transport.[1]   But, as a matter of fact, this
temple, which Livy considers the oldest in Rome, does not
appear in history till 328, when, four full centuries later,
it received the *spolia opima* of the Veian king Volumnius—
a trophy still visible in the time of Augustus.[2] The
primitive Roman rite, as Virgil knew, was either to burn
the enemy's spoils [3] or to hang them on the trunk of an
oak tree raised upon a hillock : [4] thus Aeneas ' reared
on a mound a giant oak, shorn of its encircling boughs,
and clothed it in shining arms.' [5]

I am not aware of any text which indicates that the
Romans, like the Teutons and Cimbrians, were in the
habit of throwing their spoils into lakes and marshes,
yet I believe they must have done so ; for not only did
the Italian lakes receive a quantity of offerings in the
shape of *stipites*, but, at the rebuilding of the Capitol by
Vespasian, the haruspices, who were steeped in ancient
custom, ordered the flame-scorched ruins of the old
temple to be flung into the marshes to preclude their after
use.[6]

[1] Livy, i. 10, 5.   The etymology, of course, is absurd ; the one
which connects *Feretrius* with *ferire* is more reasonable (Prop. v. 10, 46).
Cf. the art. ' Jupiter ' in Roscher's *Lexikon*, pp. 671, 674.

[2] *Cf.* Hermes, vol. xiii. p. 142.

[3] Virg. *Aen.* xi. 193.

[4] Lucan's oak, *sublimis in agro*, is ' sublime ' for this reason (*Phars.*
i. 136).

[5] ' Ingentem quercum decisis undique ramis
   constituit tumulo fulgentiaque induit arma ' (*Aen.* xi. 5).

[6] ' Ut reliquiae prioris delubri in paludes aveherentur ' (Tac. *Hist.*
iv. 53).

V

In the historical period, the Romans may well have vowed the spoils of the enemy to a particular deity beforehand, as did Fabius at the moment of his attack on the Samnites.[1] But when, by way of fulfilling their engagement, they destroyed the booty instead of preserving it, they were obeying a custom whose primitive character had been obscured by time. When, again, they saw the barbarians doing likewise, they imagined them to be offering sacrifices to their gods ; for they had lost the conception of a primitive state in which a sacrifice was something the poles removed from an offering to a given divinity. Yet, in one passage at least, Livy seems to have felt a doubt. In 176 B.C. the Ligurians took Mutina, seized an enormous amount of booty, and destroyed it. ' They killed the prisoners after hacking them to pieces, turned the temples into shambles rather than places of sacrifice,[2] and finally, after a carnage of all living things, vented their fury upon inanimate objects. Vases of every kind were dashed against the walls—especially any that seemed made for use rather than ornament.'[3] Thus the Ligurians behaved precisely as did the Cimbrians and Teutons seventy years afterwards, butchering and battering everything with such a rage of destruction that Livy hesitates to term this massacre a sacrifice—*trucidant verius quam sacrificant.* And, indeed,

---

[1] Livy, x. 29, 14–18.

[2] '. . . cum foeda laceratione interficiunt . . . pecora in fanis trucidant verius passim quam interficiunt.'

[3] Livy, xli. 18 : 'Satiati caede animantium, quae inanima erant parietibus adfligunt, vasa omnis generis usui magis quam ornamento in speciem facta. . . .' (An allusion to the destruction of the precious vases of Corinth by Mummius ?)

to call it a sacrifice would be an abuse of words : there is no question here of a gift-sacrifice, none of a sacrifice of expiation or communion ; it is simply and solely the execution of a sort of outlawry, *herem*, to use the expression of the Bible, which furnishes us with equivalent examples.

Before passing to those examples, which are exceedingly instructive, I must touch briefly on the rite whose distinctive feature is that the hostile spoils are left heaped on the ground without being burnt. I have found no text attesting its practice in Italy ; but a very important passage in Caesar attributes it to the Gauls, whose civilisation at the time of the conquest offers more than one analogy to that of primitive Italy. 'Mars,' he says,[1] ' is their arbiter of war ; and as a general rule, if they are resolved on battle, they promise him the spoils. After victory they sacrifice all animals that fall into their hands and deposit the remainder of their prizes in some one determinate place : in many districts the towering heaps of spoil on consecrated ground are very noticeable. It rarely happens that a Gaul so far defies his religion as to conceal a part of the booty in his house or to remove anything from the general pile : the penalty for that offence is death, preceded by the cruelest tortures.' Caesar rightly perceived that it was here a question of a religious law or custom, sanctioned by the most terrible penalties. Other texts tell us the Gauls sometimes burned the booty.[2] On occasion, also, they sank it in lakes or ponds—those, for instance, around Toulouse, where, in 105 B.C., the Romans under Q. Servilius Caepio

---

[1] Caesar, *Bell. Gall.* vi. 17.

[2] This must undoubtedly be Florus' meaning, when he says the Boii vowed the Roman arms to Vulcan (i. 20, 5). *Cf.* Waltzing, *Rev. des Études anciennes*, vol. iv. p. 53.

reaped an ample harvest of gold and silver.[1] The commonly received opinion that these ponds served as treasuries for the Tectosages is obviously inadmissible. Not less so is the story that their riches were fruits of the pillage of Delphi ; though there is one grain of truth in the legend : the gold of Toulouse, *aurum Tolosanum*, was the result of military expeditions, and had been submerged on account of its sacred character. I have already remarked that the sanctity of the spoils threatened the gravest consequences to those who touched or appropriated the objects thus withdrawn from circulation. Hence, when Caepio and his army were annihilated in 105 B.C. by the Cimbrians, the disaster was ascribed to the sacrilegious theft of the Toulouse gold—an opinion which must have originated in Gaul and afterwards have filtered through to Italy, where it was a commonplace that the treasure had been fatal, not only to the actual depredators, but even to their kith and kin. These are the normal effects of a violated taboo.[2]

M. d'Arbois de Jubainville has recently commented on the following well-known excerpt from Diodorus, relative to the Celts :[3] ' Taking the heads of their fallen foes, and fastening them to their horses' necks, they leave to their servants the bloody spoils of the slain, and for their sole booty carry off the scalps amid songs of triumph and hymns of victory.' M. d'Arbois justly observes that there must have been many Germans amongst these servants ; and here we have a feasible explanation how the Celtic word for victory, *bheŭdi*,

[1] Strabo, iv. 1, 13 ; Justin, xxxii. 3, 9.

[2] At a later period the Gauls, like the Romans, preserved their booty in temples. Cf. *Revue des Études anciennes*, vol. iv. pp. 280 *sq.*

[3] Diod. Sic. v. 24, 4. *Cf.* d'Arbois, *Comptes rendus de l'Acad. des Inscr.* 1907, p. 172.

became the German word *Beute*—booty.   Diodorus omits
to specify the Celtic tribe he alludes to ; and the habit he
describes cannot have been general, as it contradicts the
direct evidence of Caesar.   However, it may be retained
as an example, local perhaps, of a religious reminiscence
vivid enough to deter the Gauls from carrying off the
spoils of war.   To say they were content with the mere
glory of conquest, and nursed a chivalrous disdain for the
material fruits of victory, is to be misled by the influence
of exclusively modern ideas ; a lapse which was made by
Engelhardt, who, in the passage quoted above, attributes
a like disinterestedness to the Scandinavian warriors who
threw their booty into the lakes.   These are the domains
of superstition, not of ethics.   Only when superstition
relaxed her grip, and the desire for material emoluments
and tangible gains took the upper hand, did the dread of
touching the booty give way to the lust of possessing it.
This was the attitude of the Germans in Augustan days,
when they slaughtered the officers of Varus' army, but
did not hesitate to enrich themselves with the spoils.[1]
Tacitus, relating the avenging campaign of Germanicus,
more than once remarks upon the avidity shown by the
soldiers of Arminius 'who preferred robbery to blood.'[2]
And yet these Germans had preserved the memory of
their ancestors' habit of consecrating spoils by suspension,
a method similar to the one long practised at Rome ; for
the ensigns of Varus' legions were fixed by Arminius to
old oaks in the Teutoburger Wald.[3]

[1] Tacitus, *Ann.* i. 37 : 'Ferebantur et spolia Varianae cladis, plerisque
. . . praedae data.'
[2] *Ibid.* i. 65 : 'Hostium aviditas, omissa caede, praedam sectantium.'
[3] *Ibid.* i. 59.

VI

In order to confirm and clarify what has been said up to now with regard to the sacred character of spoils taken in warfare, and the religious objection of semi-barbarous peoples to their appropriation and subsequent use, there is no need to scour North America for examples ; the Bible is sufficient.

The theory of the interdict (*herem*), which condemns the spoil of the enemy to destruction, with a few reservations dictated by practical necessity, is found in two passages of Deuteronomy and Numbers :—

' When the Lord thy God shall bring thee into the land whither thou goest to possess it . . .; and when the Lord thy God shall deliver them before thee ; thou shalt smite them, and utterly destroy them ; thou shalt make no covenant with them, nor shew mercy unto them: neither shalt thou make marriages with them ; thy daughter thou shalt not give unto his son, nor his daughter shalt thou take unto thy son.   For they will turn away thy son from following me.' [1]

' Only the gold, and the silver, the brass, the iron, the tin, and the lead, everything that may abide the fire, ye shall make it go through the fire, and it shall be clean : nevertheless it shall be purified with the water of separation : and all that abideth not the fire ye shall make go through the water.' [2]

And now for the practice, which naturally precedes all theory. We find it in the book of Joshua.[3] The Hebrews had arrived before Jericho, only to find the gates shut. ' And the Lord said unto Joshua, See, I

[1] Deuteronomy vii. 1-4.   [2] Numbers xxxi. 22, 23.
[3] Joshua vi. 2 *sqq*.

have given into thine hand Jericho, and the king thereof, and the mighty men of valour. And ye shall compass the city all ye men of war, and go round about the city once. Thus shalt thou do six days. And seven priests shall bear before the ark seven trumpets of rams' horns : and the seventh day ye shall compass the city seven times, and the priests shall blow with the trumpets. And it shall come to pass, that when they make a long blast with the ram's horn and when ye hear the sound of the trumpet, all the people shall shout with a great shout ; and the wall of the city shall fall down flat.' Joshua hearkened to the word of the Lord, traced a *magic circle* round the town, and 'cut it off '; that is, virtually suppressed it. On the seventh day, when the seventh circuit had been made, and the priests lifted their trumpets, ' Joshua said unto the people, Shout ; for the Lord hath given you the city. And the city shall be accursed, even it, and all that are therein, to the Lord : only Rahab the harlot shall live, she and all that are with her in the house, because she hid the messengers that we sent. And ye, in any wise keep yourselves from the accursed thing lest ye make yourself accursed, when ye take of the accursed thing, and make the camp of Israel a curse, and trouble it. But all the silver and gold, and vessels of brass and iron, are consecrated unto the Lord : they shall come unto the treasury of the Lord.' The walls fell, Jericho was taken, and the Hebrews applied the interdict, killing ' both man and woman, young and old, and ox, and sheep, and ass, with the edge of the sword.' They burnt the town and all it contained except ' the silver, and the gold, and the vessels of brass and of iron ' which they put into the treasury of the house of the Lord. And Joshua adjured them in this manner : ' Cursed be the man before the Lord, that riseth up and buildeth the city Jericho : he shall lay the foundation thereof in his first-born, and in his youngest son shall be set up the gates of it.'

The curse put in Joshua's mouth appears to have borne fruit : for centuries none dare to rebuild Jericho.[1] The extensive excavations, recently carried out on the site by MM. Sellin and Niemann, have brought to light the remains of the walls and of two forts, along with a great number of broken articles, especially fragments of vases ; almost all of which, so the explorers maintain, go back to the Canaanitish period before the Hebrew supremacy. Once 'cut off' by the magic operations described, Jericho ceased to exist. The savage destruction of the town and all its contents, animate and inanimate, is strangely reminiscent of Livy's account of the Ligurian frenzy at Mutina, and of the passage in which Orosius deals with the Cimbrians ; but the sequel is yet more instructive, for it throws light on the contagion immanent in objects stricken by the *herem*. Even though the book of Joshua, in its present form, may not be earlier than the Exile, the primitive stamp of thought everywhere apparent is enough to show that the bed-rock of the narrative

---

[1] The first book of Kings (xvi. 34) relates that, in the time of Ahab, Hiel the Bethelite rebuilt Jericho, but at the price of the lives of his two sons : ' he laid the foundation thereof on Abiram his firstborn, and set up the gates thereof in his youngest son Segub, according to the word of the Lord, which he spake by Joshua the son of Nun.' This might seem the echo of a *foundation-sacrifice*, designed to buy off or blot out the *herem* ; but the text, such as it is, hints rather at an accident which cost the life of Hiel's two sons (Reuss, *La Bible*, vol. i. p. 485). Reuss remarks on the point : ' Jericho had long been rebuilt, and is mentioned as an existing and inhabited town in the story of David.' This inference is in no way to be drawn from the text cited (2 Samuel x. 5).

belongs to the remote past, when a still rudimentary civilisation was wholly dominated by religious scruples.[1]

VII

In spite of the interdict a Hebrew by the name of Achan appropriated some of the objects that came from Jericho. The sanction of the violated taboo soon made itself felt : three thousand soldiers were put to flight by the inhabitants of Ai. Joshua bowed himself before the Ark and prayed to the Lord. Then the Lord said to Joshua : 'Israel hath sinned, and they have also transgressed my covenant which I commanded them : for they have even taken of the accursed thing, and have also stolen, and dissembled also, and they have put it even among their own stuff. Therefore, the children of Israel could not stand before their enemies, but turned their backs before their enemies, because they were accursed : neither will I be with you any more, except ye destroy the accursed from among you.' Thus the whole people was contaminated by the crime of an individual ; and this crime had to be expiated, for 'there is an accursed thing in the midst of thee, O Israel.' What follows is obscure, the text being doubtless corrupt ; but it seems as though, to discover the culprit, the Lord had prescribed a magic test—an appeal to the ordeal of casting lots. The lot fell upon Achan, who acknowledged his guilt : 'When I saw among the spoils a goodly Babylonish

---

[1] The redactor of the book of Joshua makes Jahveh intervene in everything, just as the Roman historians spoke of the spoils as consecrated *to the gods* ; but 'the taboo of the spoils' with all its consequences appears to have been much earlier than the constitution of Hebraic monotheism, as well as anterior to that of Roman polytheism. It belongs to the period of magic and *djinn* (polydemonism).

garment, and two hundred shekels of silver, and a wedge of gold of fifty shekels weight, then I coveted them, and took them ; and, behold, they are hid in the earth in the midst of my tent, and the silver under it.' Joshua sent messengers to the tent of Achan, and the articles were recovered. Then, acting upon the express commands of the Lord, he seized Achan, together with the silver, the garment, the wedge of gold, his sons and his daughters, his oxen and his asses, his sheep, his tent and all his goods ; and, followed by all Israel, he led them to the valley of Achor. And Joshua said to him : ' Why hast thou troubled us ? The Lord shall trouble thee this day. And all Israel stoned him with stones, and burned them with fire, after they had stoned them with stones. And they raised over him a heap of stones unto this day. So the Lord turned from the fierceness of his anger. Wherefore, the name of that place was called, the valley of Achor (*trouble*), unto this day.'

Comparing this with the passage from Caesar, we now understand why a Gaul who purloined anything from the heap of spoils was put to a lingering death by torture. Not only did he defile himself by laying hands on the sacred and interdicted objects, but he exposed the whole community to the contagion of his own pollution. It was imperative, therefore, in the public interest, to strike terror into potential evil-doers by the most drastic examples and threats ; and the extermination of a criminal with every refinement of cruelty was held to be the surest deterrent to his would-be imitators. This idea, that the pollution was contagious, crops up in the story of the theft of the Toulouse treasure by Caepio, who was killed by the Cimbrians, his army annihilated, and his very daughters, according to Strabo, reduced to the vilest prostitution. The moral and intellectual outlook of the persons who circulated this edifying piece of history, sometime about the year 100 B.C., is little different from that of the redactor of Joshua, who calmly dilates on the sufferings of Achan, the stoning and burning of his sons and daughters, cattle and sheep, and the destruction even of his lifeless belongings, which might possibly be infected with the germ of uncleanness. Of course, the whole narrative may have been fabricated to account for the existence of a stone tumulus in a place called *Achor*, for the belief was general that a heap of stones invariably covered the body of a criminal who had been stoned to death. But the important point for the history of religion and morals is not that the events should have occurred precisely as they are related in the Bible, but that it should have been thought possible and probable for them to have so occurred.

A few years ago, M. l'abbé Paul Renard, Doctor of Theology, and professor of Holy Writ in the Grand Séminaire de Chartres, thus summarised the Achan episode : [1] 'His crime was the violation of the order of Joshua, who had expressly anathematised the town with all that it contained—both men and booty. This annihilation of the first town conquered in Canaan was a sort of religious consecration carried out, partly in acknowledgment of the sovereign rights of Jehovah, and partly to inspire a wholesome fear in the rest. Hence disobedience to the order became an act of sacrilege deserving the vengeance of God.'

This method of satisfying the requirements of modern ethics by an emasculation and distortion of the facts is a vexatious anachronism ; nor is the indignation expressed

---

[1] Vigouroux, *Dictionnaire de la Bible*, s.v. ' Akhan.'

by the philosophers of the eighteenth century, on the perusal of these barbarous narratives, less contrary to the exigencies of the critical spirit. At a certain moment of their social evolution, the Hebrews, the Ligurians, the Cimbrians, and, no doubt, all other nations as well, have thought the same and acted the same. Their deeds, though they may fill us with horror, were only the logical outcome of their ideas ; and if we feel some pride in measuring the road travelled since then, we ought to reserve our censure for those who would even now propose the conduct of prehistoric savages as a guide for our consciences and morals.

There are other examples of the laying down of an interdict in the Bible, and also of its violation. Thus Saul, despite the word of the Lord, who bade him smite the Amalekites and kill 'both man and woman, infant and suckling, ox and sheep, camel and ass,' stopped short after butchering the Amalekites, and kept the pick of their cattle. The Almighty rebuked his dis-obedience by the mouth of Samuel, and punished him for it. Saul's defence is interesting : [1] 'I . . . have utterly destroyed the Amalekites. But the people took the spoil, sheep and oxen, the chief of the things which should have been utterly destroyed, to sacrifice unto the Lord thy God in Gilgal.' As the excuse was not admitted, it follows that the enforcement of the interdict has nothing whatever in common with a sacrifice. Only things clean can be offered up to God, and the interdict is first and foremost an interdict of the unclean ; even the metal objects preserved must undergo a purification by fire and water before taking their place in the treasure-house of the Almighty. Here, in its simple and primitive form,

[1] I Samuel xv. 3; ii. 23.

we have the rite of 'outlawry,' that ban on persons and things in time of war, which we meet—anæmic now, and half anthropomorphised—in the pages of the classic historians. When these tell us that a general, before the battle, vowed the fruits of his approaching victory to this or that divinity, the Biblical *herem* allows us to penetrate the underlying principle of the act : it was not a case of oblation or sacrifice, but of extermination.

VIII

Now that we have established the nature of the *herem* and its equivalents among other nations of antiquity, we come to the second part of our inquiry. What was the origin of a custom, so directly opposed to the material and immediate interests of the poor but passively obedient tribes which it forbade to act on the sensible, if secular, axiom : *What is good to take is good to keep* ?

There is a so-called orthodox explanation of this as-semblage of facts, much favoured by the ordinary commen-tator of the Bible. ' In certain cases,' writes M. l'abbé Lesêtre, ' in order to inspire the Israelites with a horror of idolatry, God commanded that all booty taken from the idolaters should be destroyed, with the exception of what could be purified by fire,—metal objects for instance. . . . These precautions had for aim both the physical hygiene and the moral purity of the Hebrews.' [1]   The notion that the use of fire and water for the *religious* purifica-tion of metal articles from a looted town was inspired by a solicitude for ' physical hygiene ' may possibly be ingenious, but certainly does not merit discussion. As to the ' moral hygiene ' of the Israelites, it is open to question

---

[1] Vigouroux, *Dictionnaire de la Bible*, art. ' Butin.'

whether the massacre of children at the breast and women with child was peculiarly well calculated to promote it. Moreover, in such cases it is neither scientific nor even commonly honest to neglect the parallels furnished by the history of pagan nations. As the Biblical *herem* is only a particular instance of a custom, once very widely spread if not universal, no historian—though he be an orthodox theologian—has any right to allege the good intentions of the Almighty and the precautions of Divine Wisdom against the contagion of idolatry.

A German scholar, Herr Schwally, who has recently studied the holy wars of ancient Israel,[1] thinks that ' the interdict imposed on booty was only an obstacle to individual greed ; the consecration preserved the integrity of the loot.' He refers, in this connection, to the Polynesian use of the taboo for protecting the fruits before the harvest, and the products of the tribal fishing and hunting before their division.[2] In a word, the interdict is a manufactured superstition invented to fill the place of police regulations which were then impracticable. Here, at the beginning of the twentieth century, we have an hypothesis which would not have been disavowed by the Encyclopædists of the eighteenth—ready as they always were to explain the apparently most fantastic customs as the deliberate inventions of religious legislators, whom they classified as benevolent impostors from the same mint as Voltaire's Mohammed. M. Fauconnet justly remarks on this view : ' The theory of the *herem*, proposed

---

[1] F. Schwally, *Semitische Kriegsalterthümer*, I. *Der heilige Krieg im alten Israël*, Leipzig, 1901. *Cf.* Fauconnet, *Année sociologique*, vol. v. pp. 602 *sq.*

[2] Fauconnet, *loc. laud.* p. 605. The analogy between the *herem* and the taboo had been already recognised by Rob. Smith (*Religion der Semiten*, p. 118) : ' Ein solcher Bann ist ein Tabu, das durch die Furcht vor übernatürlichen Strafen veranlasst ist.'

by M. Schwally, must apparently be consigned to the same category as those other theories which would explain . . . the rules of exogamy by the drawbacks attendant on consanguineous marriages.' And, in fact, the anachronism and absurdity are not less. But I fancy M. Fauconnet's resignation is a little premature, when he says ' the causes which determined the consecration and destruction of the booty remain to be discovered.' To me they seem easy enough to fathom. With primitive mankind, war is an essentially religious phenomenon. Peace itself, not only between clansman and clansman but between clan and clan or tribe and neighbouring tribe, is based exclusively on religious ideas and religious ties. To break those ties which protect man against man—to be authorised in violating, to the detriment of a given community, the sacred scruple of human blood—you must have another religious phenomenon of equal power. And the manifestation of this is the solemn outlawry of the enemy and all that is his. In the case of Jericho we have seen that the Ark of the Covenant was carried seven times round the walls, tracing a magic circle which ' cut off ' the enemy's town, and suppressed it—ideally, of course—before a single act of overt hostility had been committed. The magic proved operative, the walls dropped, and it only remained for the Israelites to destroy by fire and sword what they had already virtually annihilated. There was no question, I repeat, of a sacrifice ; for only things clean can be offered to the gods, and a formal purification was necessary before the gold and silver of Jericho could be placed in the divine treasury. On the contrary, everything on which an interdict is laid becomes impure—with an impurity that is dangerous, not only to the individual, but—witness the story of

Achan—to the whole group of which he forms a part. From this point of view, destruction and extermination are not acts of anger and vengeance, but precautionary measures, similar, in due proportion, to those taken in our day, when an infected lazaretto is burnt and not a stick or a stone left. It is obvious, of course, that, in scenes of arson and massacre, ferocity and the wickedness of man's heart are more likely to run amok than to abdicate their claims ; but, neither in the case of the Hebrews, nor in that of the Ligurians and Cimbrians, can those passions explain the systematic destruction of cattle and even inanimate objects. Ferocity was the hand that struck, the brain which conceived and ruled was religion.

'Tantum relligio potuit suadere malorum ! '

To conclude : the spoils of war were inoculated with a magic power for evil—a virus communicated by the conqueror's own wizardry. Logic and 'magical hygiene ' alike demanded their destruction ; but covetousness sighed at the waste, and before long self-interest and the practical needs of life began to temper the iron rigours of the excommunication. And, first, with regard to human life, only the adult males were slain ; women, girls, and children were reduced to slavery, until in the end the whole vanquished population shared the same fate and swelled the riches of the victor. As for animals and lifeless objects, recourse was had to two expedients. Either the clan, following a prescribed ritual, purified all it wished to keep and use ; or it surrendered a part in return for the privilege of retaining the rest. The priesthood—omnipotent in the sphere of magic—determined alike the proportion that should be enfranchised to the conqueror, and the amount which must escheat

to the gods and remain forever untouched and unappro-
priated. Of all the objects which the victor renounced,
either to be destroyed by fire or water, or to be exposed
in a holy place beyond the reach of harm, none preserved
their inviolability so long as the *exuviae*—the arms and
personal equipment of the vanquished. But another
factor had to be reckoned with ; and, in the course of
time, national pride and individual vanity converted into
trophies of victory the weapons and harness, once gathered
together and laid away through fear of the supernatural
dangers which attached to them. When we look at the
trophies of Dacian arms sculptured on the base of Trajan's
column, it is not amiss to recall that these monuments of
military glory are only the secular outcome, so to say,
of a long process of evolution whose beginning was the
sequestration of arms taken from the enemy—a sequestration dictated by scruples eminently and exclusively
religious.

The foregoing developments at last enable me to
offer what I venture to think is a simple and convincing
explanation of one of the strangest legends in the primitive
history of Rome : I mean the death of Tarpeia.

IX

Livy's story is common knowledge.[1] The Sabines,
under King Tatius, attacked the Capitol—the Roman
fortress. The governor's daughter Tarpeia, seduced by
the sight of the gold ornaments which they wore on the
left arm, promised to betray the citadel in exchange.
However, the moment she gave them entry, they buried
her under their shields, ' either ' (says Livy) ' to create an

---

[1] Livy, i. 11 (after Fabius Pictor and Cincius Alimentus).

impression that they had taken the place by assault, or to discourage treason by a memorable example.'[1]

Many variants of the tale have come down to us ; some transmitted directly, others mentioned, only to be discarded, by the historians in general and Dionysius and Plutarch in particular. Schwegler and, more recently, Ettore Pais have taken great, perhaps too great, pains to marshal and discuss the details. It will be enough for us to show that, by the testimony of the texts themselves, every incident of the story was doubtful and fluctuating, even in antiquity, with the exception of a single point, on which our authorities speak with one voice : Tarpeia had been crushed to death under the weight of the enemy's arms. I have had occasion to point out in some of my earlier articles that the same phenomenon recurs in several old legends whose theme is the violent death of a hero : the causes, remote or proximate, of the catastrophe are lost in a tangle of conflicting traditions or gross inconsistencies ; agreement exists only as to the actual circumstances of the death. The conclusion is forced upon us from the outset : these stories and the like have their origin in self-conscious combination, and the parent stem of the various ætiologies is the one tangible reality for us—a cult or a ritual.

A glance at the variants of the Tarpeian legend shows the following results :—

1. The majority of writers place the heroine in the reign of Romulus ; but the Greek poet Simylus would have it that she betrayed the Capitol to the Gauls under Brennus.[2]

---

[1] 'Obrutam armis necavere, seu ut vi capta potius arx videretur, seu prodendi exempli causa, ne quid unquam fidum proditori esset' (Livy, i. 11, 7). Analogous reflections in Plut. *Rom.* xvii. 7, and Prop. v. 4, 89.

[2] *Ap.* Plut. *Rom.* xvii.

2. Most historians make her a Roman, but some say that she was a Sabine.[1]

3. According to some, her father, Tarpeius, was absent ; others describe him as a traitor put to death by Romulus.[2]

4. The custody of the citadel belonged, according to some, to Tarpeius ; according to others, to Tarpeia herself.[3]

5. Tarpeia was or was not a Vestal Virgin.[4]

6. According to some, she acted from cupidity ; [5] according to others, to entrap the Sabines by exacting the surrender of their shields ; [6] according to Propertius, she was in love with Tatius ; [7] according to Simylus, with Brennus ; [8] according to Antigonus of Carystus, she wished to be avenged upon Romulus.[9]

7. The Sabines (or the Gauls) killed her, either to foster the belief that they had penetrated into the citadel by force, or from disgust at her treason,[10] or to punish her for deceiving them, or to escape parting with their golden ornaments,[11] or because she refused to reveal the secrets of Romulus to Tatius.[12]

All are unanimous on the one point that Tarpeia was crushed under the arms and ornaments of the enemy.

---

[1] Antigonus of Carystus made her the daughter of Tatius (Plut. *Rom.* xvii.).

[2] Opinion of Sulpicius Galba ; combated by Plut. *Rom.* xvii.

[3] Another opinion refuted by Plutarch (*l.l.*).

[4] She was a Vestal Virgin according to Varro (*L. Lat.* v. 41), Propertius (v. 4, 18), and the chronographer of 354 (*Chron. Min.* i. p. 144, 8). Those who say that she met the Sabines while going out to draw water seem to share the same opinion (Livy, i. 11 ; Val. Max. ix. 6, 1, &c.).

[5] Livy, i. 11.

[6] The version of L. Calpurnius Piso, adopted by Dionysius (ii. 50).

[7] Prop. iv. 4, 39.   [8] Plut. *Rom.* xviii.

[9] *Ibid.*   [10] Livy, i. 11.

[11] The version of Fabius (Dionysius, ii. 38).

[12] *Chron. Min.* i. p. 144.

Almost all, in this connection, mention the great shields ; some add the golden bracelets and rings worn by the Sabines or Gauls.[1]

There is one valuable piece of numismatic evidence. In the last century of the Republic, two Roman families claiming a Sabine descent placed the virgin Tarpeia upon their coins. On the reverse side of those struck by the Titurii, she is represented in the act of separating a Roman and a Sabine warrior ; the inference being that she was considered as one of those heroic dames who threw themselves between the two armies in order to end the struggle. On the coins of the Turpilii, she is a young girl, seen from the front, with both arms raised and only the upper part of her body emerging fom a heap of shields.[2]

Thus the opinion, that Tarpeia was a Sabine and not a Roman, had its adherents in the sixth century A.U.C. The explanation is possibly to be found in the incontestable traces of a Sabine domination on the Capitol ;[3] where not only was the house of Tatius shown,[4] but it had been necessary to *exaugurate* and demolish several Latin chapels of his foundation, at the time when the temple of Jupiter was being built by Tarquin.[5] But it was sheer guesswork that translated Tarpeia into a Sabine or the daughter of Tatius himself ; positive knowledge

[1] According to Plutarch (*Rom.* xvii.) Tatius was the first to throw his shield and bracelet on Tarpeia ; and the same version—given by Piso—is familiar to Dionysius (ii. 38). In a fragment of Appian (*De Reg.* 4), quoted by Suidas and perhaps incomplete, she is buried (κατεχώσθη) under ornaments of gold. A similar account, from the suspect Aristides of Miletus, is preserved by Plutarch (*Parall.* xv.).

[2] Babelon, *Monnaies de la Rép. rom.* ii. pp. 301, 498 ; Pais, *Ancient Legends of Roman History*, p. 97.

[3] Liv. i. 32 ; Tac. *Ann.* xii. 24 ; Dionys. ii. 50.

[4] Plut. *Rom.* 20 ; Solin. i. 21.

[5] Livy, i. 55. *Cf.* Schwegler, *Röm. Gesch.* i. p. 484.

of her there was none, beyond these three facts : a
rock on the Capitol was called by her name, her tomb—
or cenotaph—was exhibited there, and yearly rites were
celebrated in her honour.   This follows unmistakably
from the passage in which Dionysius subscribes to the
version given in the Gracchan period by Calpurnius Piso,
who held that Tarpeia had not betrayed the Romans, but
attempted to deceive their enemies.   ' The sequel of the
incident,' says Dionysius,[1] ' demonstrates the truth of
Piso's view ;   for a magnificent tomb was erected to
Tarpeia on the holiest of the Seven Hills, at the place
where she met her death ; and every year—to repeat Piso
—the Romans make libations and offer sacrifices to her.
Now, it is certain that, had she perished in the act of
selling her country to the enemy, neither those who
killed her nor those whom she betrayed would have
shown her any such respect, but rather have flung her
carcass into the sewer.'   Plutarch seems to imply that
this tomb was a cenotaph, or, strictly speaking, an altar
more than a tomb.   ' Tarpeia,' he says,[2] ' was buried in
this very place and the hill took its name *Tarpeian*
from her, until King Tarquin consecrated it to Jupiter ; [3]
when her remains were transferred elsewhere, and her
name disappeared (καὶ τοὔνομα τῆς Ταρπηίας ἐξέλιπε).
One trace, however, was left ; and the rock on the
Capitol, from which condemned criminals are hurled to
their death, is still known as the Tarpeian Rock.'
Now, if Tarpeia's remains had really been ' transferred

---

[1] Dionysius, ii. 38.   [2] Plut. *Rom.* xvii.

[3] Mr. Pais thinks the name *Tarpeia* identical with *Tarquin*,
and considers the Vestal Tarpeia and the Vestal Tarquinia, who
gave the plain of the Tiber to the Romans, to be one and the
same person (*Legends of Roman History*, p. 105).   The theory seems
to me inadmissible.

elsewhere,' vestiges of her cult would have been dis-covered somewhere in Rome. But the case is not so ; and the passage from Plutarch is probably the echo of a lost text which stated the negative results of a search for the maiden's bones. Finally, Festus puts it on record that current opinion recognised Tarpeia in an old statue in the temple of Jupiter built by Metellus (*in aede Jovis Metellina*).[1] Unfortunately, he enters into no detail, and we can hardly suppose the image to have been similar to that on the Turpilian coins.

This latter, then, is our only document ; and we may take it as the starting-point in our attempt to determine what the ancients definitely knew—or believed them-selves to know—upon the subject, and to unravel the tangled skein of legends designed to account for one feature or another in the tale.

X

Tarpeia was the local divinity of the Tarpeian Rock ; and there she possessed an altar where her cult was annually celebrated. Tradition had it that she died on this spot, crushed to death by shields—Sabine in some versions, Gaulish in others, but in either case *non-Roman*. The engraver of the coin represented her agony, while she was still writhing under the weight of the arms accumu-lated upon her ; a moment later, and nothing would have been visible but a heap of shields in the form of a mound. Now, this mound of shields, which quite possibly was interspersed with a few rings, bracelets, and armlets of gold, is the root of the whole legend ; and after what has been said above, it is easy to account for its existence.

[1] Festus, p. 363, M.

At a period when temples were still to seek at Rome, and huts served for houses, the spoils of war, so far as they escaped destruction, must—like the Gaulish trophies noticed by Caesar—have been piled on some plot of consecrated ground, where they were immune from touch. In these heaps of arms the trophy had its origin ; and Tacitus, speaking of that erected by Germanicus, could still call it a 'mound of weapons.'[1]   But with the advent of temples and comparatively large dwelling-houses where the enemy's spoil might be hung, the primitive rite was forgotten, and the pile of shields on the Tarpeian Hill became an enigma.   Now, with ancient as well as modern man, the sight of a heap of stones is certain to engender the belief that an important personage lies buried beneath—generally as a punishment for some crime.   I could cite many examples from latter-day folklore ; but there is no dearth of classical texts.   An epigram on the brigand Balista, attributed to Virgil, begins :

'Under this hill of stones Balista lies.'[2]

Achilles caused Pisidice of Methymna to be crushed under a heap of stones.[3]   In the days which saw the compilation of the book of Joshua, the heap of stones under which Achan [4] slept was still pointed out, as well as another that covered the body of the King of Ai.[5]   Possibly the fact that stoning to death was the usual penalty for the most serious crimes may have favoured the birth of these legends ; but similar tales are found where it is purely a question of ordinary earthen tumuli which might be

---

[1] Tac. *Ann.* ii. 22 : 'Congeriem armorum struxit superbo cum titulo.'
[2] 'Monte sub hoc lapidum tegitur Balista sepultus' : Serv. ad *Aen.* vol. i. p. 1, ed. Thilo.
[3] Parthenius, *Erot.* xxi. 8.   [4] Joshua vii. 26.   [5] *Ibid.* viii. 29.

natural phenomena, defensive fortifications, or the sites of a cult, but are almost always regarded as the tombs of heroes or heroines, giants, fairies, and so forth. Specimens of this nomenclature, implying a whole legend, are met with in the Iliad.[1]

Popular imagination is essentially logical, even in its errors. The sight of a heap of shields, forming a tumulus on a place sacred to the cult of the eponymous heroine Tarpeia, was bound to suggest the idea that this heroine had been crushed to death under the shields. But why such a punishment ? Popular imagination is more than logical; it is just, and requires that every penalty shall have its corresponding crime. In this case, the punishment must have been inflicted by foreign warriors, for the arms employed were foreign. But warriors spare unarmed women ; therefore Tarpeia could not have been killed in defence of the Capitol. There remained the hypothesis of treason—a conjecture facilitated by the knowledge that condemned traitors (as Plutarch does not fail to recall) were hurled from the Tarpeian Rock.[2] Why, then, it may be objected, does tradition not mete out the same fate to the arch-traitress herself ? The answer is that the legend of her treason was not formed independently, but was suggested, as we have seen, by the existence of a heap of shields, under which Tarpeia, the local nymph, was buried.

If at the time of the capture of Rome by the Gauls, there existed a mound of Sabine shields on some one point of the Capitol, those arms must have disappeared in the catastrophe of 390 and have been replaced, a little later, by Gaulish weapons. This explains, to my mind, the

[1] *Il.* ii. 811–814.
[2] Plut. *Rom.* xvii. ; *Syll.* x. ; Livy, xxv. 7, 14, &c.

curious variant of the legend, according to which Tarpeia falls in love with Brennus, betrays the Capitol to the Gauls, and is whelmed under their arms. Nor is this the only feature of the story which is connected both with the Sabines and the Gauls. The little gate of the Capitol—the *Porta Pandana*[1]—had always to be left open ; but our authorities differ as to whether this was a condition of peace imposed by the Sabine Tatius[2] or an exaction of Brennus the Gaul.[3]

A detail which astonished Schwegler was the quantity and beauty of the gold ornaments attributed to the Sabines ; he suspected a confusion between them and the Gauls, whose weakness for decorative effect was notorious.[4] Mr. Pais counters the objection by pointing out that the *armillae* and rings of gold were equally appropriate to the Sabines, whose wealth in the precious metals was eulogised by Fabius Pictor, and whose arms, in 310 and 293 B.C., are described as glittering with gold and silver.[5] However, as the ancient world was always impressed by the size of the Gaulish shields, I am inclined to fancy that the legend owes its inception to the sight of a pile of them intermixed with the gold ornaments worn by the Celts on their campaigns. But, as a tradition, which we are justified in considering historical, reported a Sabine occupation of the Capitol long before the Gallic invasion, two rival legends—Gaulish and

---

[1] Paulus Diaconus, p. 220 ; *cf.* Varr. *Ling. lat.* v. 42 ; Solinus, i. 13 ; Arnobius, iv. 3.

[2] Festus, p. 363 : ' When making peace, Tatius insisted that the gate should always be open to the Sabines'—*ut ea Sabinis semper pateret.*

[3] Polyaen. viii. 25, 1.

[4] Livy, vii. 10 ; Gell. ix. 11, 5 ; xiii. 3, 7 ; Pliny, xxiii. 5, 15, &c.

[5] Pais, *Ancient Legends*, p. 298 ; *cf.* Plut. *Cat. maior*, ii. 2 ; Livy, ix. 40 ; x. 39.

Sabine—sprang up, the second of which won the more general acceptance, partly because it referred to a more distant period, and partly, perhaps, because the Sabine conquest evoked the less painful memories at Rome. Schwegler writes : ' The nature of the death assigned to Tarpeia has undoubtedly a local reason which cannot be divined,'[1] and Mr. Pais has, more recently, come to the same conclusion. I believe I have shown that the problem may be solved without allowing hypothesis to play too great a part.

XI

When it was a question of crystallising and fixing the literary form of the Tarpeian legends, the historians drew upon the treasury of Greek fable ; and there they found all the analogies they desired. In the first place, there was a whole string of stories dealing with fair and frail ladies who betrayed their relatives, or who delivered up their cities in order to pleasure the object of their affections.[2] Other narratives wear a closer resemblance to the one which finally gained the day in the case of Tarpeia. The most interesting is that of Pisidice, daughter of the king of Methymna in the island of Lesbos. Achilles was besieging the town, when the princess, catching sight of him from the battlements, lost her heart, and sent out her nurse, offering to sell the town in exchange for his love. The hero promised all ; but, once master of Methymna, bade his soldiers stone the girl to death. In this connection, Parthenius[3] repeats the lines of some poet (perhaps Apollonius Rhodius, as K. Müller

---

[1] Schwegler, *Röm. Gesch.* vol. i. p. 487.
[2] Paris, *op. laud.* p. 299 ; *cf.* Schwegler, *Röm. Gesch.* vol. i. p. 484.
[3] Parthenius, *Erotica*, xxi.

conjectured), who sang the early history of Lesbos in hexameters. There is some reason to think the legend was already known to Hesiod,[1] which, of course, excludes the idea that it might have been borrowed from that of Tarpeia. This is not the case with the story of Brennus at Ephesus, as related in the 'Parallelae'—falsely attributed to Plutarch—on the strength of a *soi-disant* 'History of the Galatians' (Γαλατικά) by Clitophon.[2] The Gaulish chief Brennus, while ravaging Asia, laid siege to Ephesus. There he succumbed to the charms of a young Greek girl, who promised to comply with his desires and betray Ephesus to boot, if she might have an equivalent in gold collars and ornaments. Brennus ordered his men to throw all the gold they had into the lap of this mercenary light-of-love ; they obeyed, and she was buried alive under the gauds. The story contrives to be both revolting and absurd : the girl could not promise her love-sick Gaul the town-keys *over and above* her favours ; there must have been an older and more rational version in which she fell in love with Brennus, as Pisidice with Achilles. But it is well known how little value can be attached to the extracts from authors, real or mythical, which fill the 'Parallelae Minores' that pass under Plutarch's name. The story of Polycrite of Naxos inspires more confidence, as it was known already to Aristotle.[3] Polycrite won the love of Diognetus, the chief of the Erythræans besieging Naxos, and exploited her conquest by opening the camp-gates to her countrymen. After the slaughter, she returned in triumph to her native town, but was suffocated under the garlands showered upon her by her fellow-

---

[1] *Cf.* Höfer, in Roscher's *Lexikon*, art. 'Peisidike,' p. 1793
[2] Pseudo-Plut. *Parall. Min.* c. xv.
[3] *Cf.* Höfer's article 'Polykrite,' in Roscher's *Lexikon*, p. 2650.

citizens, who then erected a tomb in her honour. Though the circumstances are all different, this pretty story comprises four elements—a siege, a love intrigue, a betrayal, and the suffocation of the traitress—which are found in at least one version of the story of Tarpeia.

XII

Thus, once again, though by devious ways, I have shown how a rite gave birth to a myth. Here the rite is a taboo of the spoils of war—the custom of upheaping them on consecrated ground, where to touch them was sacrilege. The myth is that of the local heroine—the *genius loci* (for there is no place without its genius, as Servius says)—suffocated under this pile of weapons to atone for some imagined crime. Euhemerism is right, every legend has its root in reality; but if the legend is old, then the reality that gave it life is not an episode of history but a ritual—a cult-practice.

This is the end of this publication.

Any remaining blank pages are for our book binding
requirements and are blank on purpose.

To search thousands of interesting publications like this one,
please remember to visit our website at:

http://www.kessinger.net

CPSIA information can be obtained
at www.ICGtesting.com
Printed in the USA
LVHW012100140120
643609LV00013B/354

9 781162 884004